LOUDER!

The Official James Scott
Loud Reading Poetry Book

Poems By James Scott
Illustrations By Mary Britt

"Howard & The Pickle" was previously published in the January 1994 issue of the Sout
Coast Poetry Journal.

Second printing 1995.

LOUDER!!!

ISBN # 1-886080-00-3

DEDICATION

To my daughter Katelyn Elizabeth Scott
who helps me find the quiet joy in every loud day.

SPECIAL THANKS

To my friends who made the first printing of this book possible:

Cindy Hardy

Kevin O'Brien

Linda Price, Rebekkah & Aaron

Ruth & Bobby Jones

Shelley & John Martin

H. Kirk Williams

Dayle Horne

Errol Plata, Jr.

Judi Meyer

Nancy Rosenblatt

Vicki Brothers

Nora Jump-Scott & Justin

Grey Matter & Company

Mr. & Mrs. James W. Scott, Sr. (Mom & Dad)

Alice Swander

Pauline Faneuf

Ed & Sondra Rosequist

Sherrie Slate

Janie Clark & Marvin Sylvest

Wanda & Mickey Brooks

Joel Rubin

Barbara Parker

Bob & Terry Conwell

Peppy & Morna Owens

Jackie "Hula Hoop" Kendall

Canda & Bob Lambert

Ilona Brown & Wesley

The Haddads--Mary, Lou, Sammy, David, & Diana

Millard & Suzy Arnold

Brian & Jane Scott

Bill Salmon & Miki Meekins

ELBOW PAIN

I hit my elbow on the door,
It made me scream in pain.
"OW!" I said, "OW! OW! OW! OW!"
And "OW! OW! OW!" again.
"What's wrong, my son?" my mother said,
"Did you hit your funny bone, honey?"
"I hit a bone," I told my mom,
"But it isn't very funny!"
I yelled and danced around the room,
Turned six somersaults and a half;
Then I figured out why it's called the 'funny bone'--
Everyone else in the room gets a big laugh!

1.

HUNGRY

I ate my cat this morning,
I ate my bird last night,
I ate my turtle for yesterday's lunch,
After my ferret tasted just right.

Last week I ate my snake,
Week before, I ate my frog;
Last month I ate seventeen gerbils;
Why won't my momma buy me a dog?

ROOMMATE

I am a monster, your closet's my home,

When your room gets dark, that's when I roam;

I make all the roof creaks that sound like feet

That your mom says are just boards swelling in the heat.

That scratchy little noise she says is a twig,

Is me and my hands, in the wall where we dig.

And that sound that she says is "Just the wind, dear"

Is me and my train, playing loud so you'll hear.

And sometimes when it sounds like your room explodes,

It's just me, in the corner, blowin' my nose.

And if you hear steps while you're tryin' to sleep,

It's just me walkin' round on my monster feet.

Yes, I work in the dark, fillin' you with fright,

'Cause you wouldn't be scared if it was daylight.

No matter how loud I would howl or cry,

This monster in your closet's only one inch high!

3.

STRANGER

Johnny was a pretty smart guy; he got good grades in school.

Then one day something happened, made Johnny look like a fool.

A grown-up offered Johnny a ride; Johnny'd never seen him before.

He got a candy bar, and he got in the car,

Now we'll never see Johnny no more.

And everybody says...

"Bye-bye, Johnny, bye-bye," where did Johnny go?

He said, "I'll take it" to a stranger when he should've said "No!"

Anyone you don't know is a stranger -- anytime, anyplace, anywhere.

They could look mean, or look like a bean, or the guy on "Double Dare."

Susie came over when this lady called to her, "Hey, Sue!"

She seemed like a friend, but that was the end, now her folks don't know
what to do.

And everybody says...

"Bye-bye, Susie, bye-bye," where did Susie go?

She said, "I'll come with you" to a stranger when she should've said "No!"

4.

An old man as old as his grandpa called Jamal one day,

He said, "Your mama's in the hospital--we've got to go right away!"

Jamal forgot what his mama said 'bout strangers lyin' like thieves.

Off went Jamal, and that was all; he's gone like the summer breeze.

And everybody says...

"Bye-bye, Jamal, bye-bye," where did Jamal go?

He said, "Take me there" to a stranger when he should've said "No!"

Say "No!" to people that you don't know, just as their words are startin',

'Cause unless you're a cow, I don't wanna see your face on any milk carton.

If you say "No!", and they say "No!", and everybody runs away,

Then that nice-looking, nice-talking stranger can't hurt anybody today.

And everybody says...

"Bye-bye, stranger, bye-bye," where did that stranger go?

There wouldn't be any more missing kids if every kid would say "No!"

No, there wouldn't be any more missing kids if every kid would say "No!"

DINOSAUR KID

My baby brother wished he was a dinosaur,
Each day he would wish it maur and maur,
So I told him, since I'm kind of a wizard,
That he should start acting like a 'terrible lizard'.
For those who don't know, 'terrible lizard' is
What 'dinosaur' means—that's from me, The Wiz.

So, I had him make big footprints in the mud;
They have to be big, or they'll all be a dud.
Then I taught him to eat bushes out in the yard,
That's what dinosaurs did—and it wasn't too hard.
He tried knocking down trees and stomping on bugs.
But he hurt his shoulders and made spots on the rugs.

I thought he would be the best dino of all,
His feet are so big and his brain is so small,
He hangs in the mud and he likes eating plants,
And if the weather is hot then he never wears pants.
One thing he could not do, no matter how hard I'd think--
I never could get him to go act extinct.

MY POEM ABOUT RAIN

I hate the rain

It is a pain

It soaked my clothes

And drenched my brain.

One more time, I should explain,

I really, really hate the rain.

I love the rain

It makes a stain

It turns my dirt

To mud again.

And one more time, I should explain,

I really, really love the rain.

I hate the rain

And love it too,

So, when it rains,

I'm so confused.

It's good and bad and fun and pain,

I love-hate-love this mean old rain.

AT THE ICE CREAM STORE

Vanilla, fudge ripple, and then cherry garden
(On a sundae I belched and then begged someone's pardon),
Some pale lemon custard and raspberry twirl
(The hair on my stomach then started to curl),
Butter almond and chocolate and burgundy cherry,
Butter brickle, banana, and cordial blackberry;
I slowly ingested each flavor exalted
And washed them all down with a chocolate malted.

Some swiss-chocolate-almond, a large dish of peach,
The whipped cream and hot fudge and nuts within reach.
Black walnut and chocolate marshmallow came then,
And I sighed a huge sigh as I shovelled them in.
Pineapple crunch and some chocolate chip
(The chaser for those: lime sherbet—triple dip),
To my insides I seemed like some kind of Godzilla
As I swallowed strawberry and cherry vanilla.

"Stop!" screamed my brain, "Or you just might get sick!"
But I downed butterscotch and some peppermint stick
My dad says that I ought to have my mouth glued shut,
Then bubble gum, mint chocolate chip, and fudge nut.
When everyone in the store had their hopes I would quit,
I topped it all off with a big banana split.
It was covered with syrup and cherries and jelly,
And it wallowed inside of my overstuffed belly.

I made a big bet that every flavor I'd eat
Without anything happening badly to me.
I added one tiny Tic-Tac to my tummy so loaded,
Took one step for the door, and promptly exploded!

CLARENCE'S STORY

Today, let me tell you of Clarence, a boy
Who'd rather have pets 'stead of having a toy.
So, while in the forests and meadows one day,
He picked up some friends as he went on his way.

In his front pants pocket, a roomy abode,
He placed one wild, wide, wimbly-warted old toad.
He picked up some lizards, so scaly and quick,
Threw them in a pocket (with mud, so they'd stick).

A small quiv'ring mouse he had chased from its lair,
Some spiders came 'long to spin webs in his hair.
Two snakes and a serpent, don't ask which is which,
A fistful of worms that he found in a ditch.

A slimy green frog 'bout the size of your fist,
And forty-eight tadpoles he couldn't resist.
A big salamander, a hill full of ants
(His pockets were full, he dropped them in his pants).

And centipedes, millipedes, bees that were drones,
Horseflies and dragonflies, beetles and stones,
Termites and weevils and mystery bugs,
And bloodworms and grubworms and slithery slugs.

His pockets, his hair, and his arms occupied,
Our young friend went home to his dear mommy's side,
She said, "Thanks, my dear son, what a good boy are you!
Fresh meat for our Halloween Slithery Stew!"

PIG OUT ON BOOKS

Here is a poem about a pig,
It really isn't very big--
The poem, that is, not the pig--
The pig is bigger than a fig,
And a whole lot fatter than a twig.
The pig will use his nose to dig,
In mud his face will zag and zig,
To find something to chew or swig.
But, if digging is your gig,
Don't dig in mud like Zig the Pig,
But, to a bookshelf drive your rig,
Pull down a book, untie your wig;
And, you could ride a Russian MIG,
Or mutiny against Captain Queeg,
And dig your way out of the brig.

Pig Out on Books--be sure you read 'em!
Pig Out on Books--does not mean eat 'em!

TOUCAN

The toucan's bill has lots of colors,

My nose has only one.

My nose looks handsomer on my face,

But his looks like a lot more fun.

THE MULBERRY POEM

Eating them mulberries all day long,
That's the big reason that I wrote this song.
Mulberry, mulberry, growing in a tree;
Mulberry, mulberry, tasty as can be.

I eat 'em til my clothes are the color of a grape,
I hang around that tree like a big purple ape.
There's purple on my nose and purple on my eyes,
There's purple on my ankles and purple on my thighs,
There's purple on my teeth and where my elbow's bent,
My belly button's even full of purple lint!
Mulberry, mulberry, growing in a tree;
Mulberry, mulberry, tasty as can be.

The juice goes in my shoes and down into my socks,
It's dripping on the dirt and it's dripping on the rocks;
The juice runs in my shirt and down inside my pants,
It's got me doing that old juicy mulberry dance;
Where you step and splish and clap and squoosh,
And everything you touch gets covered with juice.
Mulberry, mulberry, growing in a tree;
Mulberry, mulberry, tasty as can be.

I go in the house and give my momma a hug;
She says, "Did you just track that purple on my rug?"
Then she looks at her dress where I hugged her so warm,
And there's a purple stamp of me on the front of my mom!
She grabs my by my purple wrist and puts me in the tub,
She says, "You need a bath and be sure that you scrub!"
Mulberry, mulberry, growing in a tree;
Mulberry, mulberry, tasty as can be.

he comes back up once an hour's gone by,

he tub's all purple and so am I!

he scrubs with a washcloth and she scrubs with a brush,

She scrubs 'til my skin feels like purple mush;

Then she got some steel wool and she used that, too!

And all that I could say was "Ah!" and "Oooh!".

Mulberry, mulberry, growing in a tree,

Mulberry, mulberry, tasty as can be.

She couldn't get it off and her face was looking meaner,

Then she took me on down to the corner dry cleaner.

She said, "Clean this boy 'cause he's really been wicked!"

And she gave me to the man and he handed her a ticket.

"He'll be ready after five on the seventh of March."

"Be sure and get the purple out and don't use any starch!"

Mulberry, mulberry, growing in a tree,

Mulberry, mulberry, tasty as can be.

He put me on that rack in back, and then out on a truck;

They sprayed me with some chemicals that really smelled like yuck!

But they got all the purple off, I don't know where it went.

They even cleaned and they pressed all my belly button lint!

But my momma lost the ticket, she put it down some place;

She found it after I'd been waiting five whole days.

Mulberry, mulberry, growing in a tree,

Mulberry, mulberry, tasty as can be.

My momma got me home and she set me down,

And five minutes later I could not be found.

And where do you think that she fin'lly found me?

I was stuffing my face at the mulberry tree!

Mulberry, mulberry, you're my only friend;

Mulberry, mulberry, here we go again!

DON'T DO DRUGS

There's a great big meeting at the City Hall,
All the girls and boys came out;
They've got great big banners up on the wall,
Lots of parents in the crowd.
Seems the kids got tired of shakin' their heads
And waitin' for grown-ups to do it instead;
They called this meeting; put up banners that read:
"Don't Do Drugs!"

Don't Do Drugs; I'm telling you right now;
You can do a dance, or do a shirt,
Or do an impression of your best friend Bert
But you're gonna get dead, in jail, or hurt,
So Don't Do Drugs.

The first to speak was a girl of nine,
With a tear up in her eye.
She said, "My big brother thought that drugs were fine,
He was always flying high.
Then one day he flew just a bit too far,
Threw himself in front of a speeding car.
Big brother, I miss you, wherever you are!"
Don't Do Drugs.

Don't Do Drugs, I'm telling you right now;

Do macrame or a TV show;

Tell your old pal Ernie I said "Hello"

But, if you wanna get smarter and you wanna grow,

Don't Do Drugs!

All the kids took their turns at speaking out,

Told the grown-ups to get on the stick.

Where drugs crawled in, they wanted them out,

And they wanted them out real quick.

They said, "We can keep 'em out of the schools;

The kids sellin' drugs ain't nothin' but fools;

Their ex-customers have a new set of rules:

Don't Do Drugs!"

So, Don't Do Drugs, I'll tell you one more time.

Do an armpit noise or an ugly face

Do a voice like an alien in outer space,

But, if you want to live life with a smile on your face,

And you want your home and school to be a happy place,

Say it LOUD with me, let 'em hear you in space...

DON'T DO DRUGS!!

17.

HAPPY BIRTHDAY
(written for a teacher that I know)

You say today's your birthday,

        so I'm wishing you good che

It's time to celebrate,

        although you won't tell us what y

But, don't eat too much birthday cake,

        or else you might get f

And, don't go riding in a car,

        or you might get a fl

And, don't eat ice cream,

        it will make your fillings freeze in po

And, don't you try to go outside,

        all day it's s'posed to ra

And, don't go out without your gloves,

        or you might get the fl

And, don't you celebrate,

        with anything that's fun for yo

And, don't go dancing,

        you might break your leg or tear your dre

And, don't throw yourself a party,

        you'll just have to clean the mes

And, don't eat pork or Chinese food,

        or fat, or starch, or slime

Just try to follow all these rules--

18.

        and have a real good tim

LOUDER!!!

am a monster, that is what I said--

have a monster's hairy hands, and a monster's head.

OUDER!

am a Monster, that is what I said.

have a Monster's hairy hands, and a Monster's head!

OUDER!!

AM A MONSTER! THAT IS WHAT I SAID!

HAVE A MONSTER'S HAIRY HANDS! AND A MONSTER'S HEAD!

OUDER!!!

AM A MONSTER!!! THAT IS WHAT I SAID!!!

HAVE A MONSTER'S HAIRY HANDS!!! AND A MONSTER'S HEAD!!!

LOUDER!!!!

I--i am a monster, that is what i said--

now I have laryngitis, and i'm going to bed.

good night.

19.

CATERPILLAR MILLER

There once was a wooly caterpillar,
Business card said his name was Miller;
In the insect world he was a thriller,
Cute as Michael, mean as Godzilla.
Yes, Miller Caterpillar was a handsome fellow;
With a whole lot of legs and wool of bright yellow.
"Purple, yellow, green, and blue,
I think my color's better than you!"

Our Miller hung out with his yellow amigos,
Trying to act like some ornery banditos,
If we walked onto their leaves they would greet us,
Each wearing twelve pairs of tiny Adidas;
Yellow caterpillars were the only ones they liked;
Other fellow caterpillars they told to "take a hike."
"Purple, yellow, green, and blue,
I think my color's better than you!"

Yellow 'pillars didn't like purple or green,
They'd stop eating and just stand there and scream;
Then the purple and green would stand and look mean;
Each color caterpillar thought they were supreme.
On side-by-side plants, each group tried to look madder,
Hating all others and acting badder and badder.
"Purple, yellow, green, and blue,
I think my color's better than you!"
20.

hen, one day, while each claimed they were super;
icking up their legs like some Koopa Troopa,
ach hateful insect got knocked for a looper,
When each caterpillar turned into a pupa.
Yes, all of the 'pillars, both boyis and gallis,
ecame a cocoon, also called a chrysalis.
Purple, yellow, green, and blue,
think my color's better than you!"

everal months later, once each pupa grew,
Miller looked at himself, and his buddies, too;
hey had wings and could fly, and something else new--
very 'pillar was crystal, like glass clear through.
he colors were gone, so the hating all stopped,
And they flew off together to a high mountaintop.
Purple, yellow, green, and blue,
On the inside I'm just the same as you!
urple, yellow, blue, and green,
We're all the same, and we're all supreme!"

SAMMY SNAKE

I'm Sammy Snake, I do not quake;
I slither and I slide.
I slink along the sod, you see,
Across the grass I glide.

As Sammy Snake, I do not make
The slightest sort of sound.
But people scream all sorts of sounds
Whenever I am found.

I sense things with this tongue of mine,
It sticks out somewhat often.
I use it to smell, or see, or hear,
But not for lickin' or coughin'.

Please let me slide into your socks
Someday when you are seated;
Or in your sleeping bag or shed,
Or someplace nice and heated.

Treat me superb and sensibly,
With no scratch or scar or blister,
And sometime soon I'll let you sneak
And throw me at your sister!

HOWARD

(...ment for a pickle player who choked on his instrument at Carnegie Hall.)

...re is a poem to my dear friend Howard,
...ho used to play tunes on a pickle.
...'d sit there a-blowin' all night in some tavern
...d sometimes get only a nickel.
...t they buried my friend in the cold dirt this mornin',
...r vegetables I'll hold a grudge,
...hen I think of an artist cut down in his prime
...' a pickle that just wouldn't budge.

...es, he'd sound like a seven-foot-wide whoopee cushion,
...s he'd play on that altered cucumber;
...nd, just when you'd think he would have to go rest,
...meone would say, "Blow me a number!"
...t they buried my friend in the cold dirt this mornin',
...' my garden I'll plant no more dill;
...r, who would've thought that an oversized gherkin
...'ould turn on his master and kill.

...es, Howard is gone, he has been tucked away,
...ll neat in his little sarcophagus;
...ut, I still see him falling at Carnegie Hall,
...'ith that green beast jammed in his esophagus.
...ut they buried my friend in the cold dirt this mornin',
...nd his grave was with flowers embellished;
...'es, we laid him out nice, and we set him down fin...
...nd we chopped that jammed pickle to relish.

23.

TELEVISION, TELEVISION

There once was a girl, and her name was Tess,
And her parents didn't want her to make a mess;
So, they put her in front of the television set,
And they told her to watch every channel she could get.

Though they wouldn't let her go outside for fun,
There was fun to see on Channel One.
When she thought that she might want something else to do,
They made her watch scary movies on Channel Two.

And when the movies were too scary to see,
There were business reports on Channel Three.
Soon the business reports became a bore,
So,there was all-day sports on Channel Four.

But she didn't want to watch some old high dive,
So she caught cartoons on Channel Five.
Once she recognized all of Coyote's tricks,
She switched to shopping on Channel Six.

So she ordered a genuine Barney plate,
Then zapped right through Channels Seven and Eight.
Nine was the Fishing Channel, then she squirmed,
When she saw all the ways you could cut up a worm.

Channels Ten and Eleven were nothing but news,
If she stayed there long, she would take a big snooze.
Channel Twelve was wrestling, day and night,
And she liked the make-up, and she liked the tights.

The all-gum channel was Channel Thirteen,
Watching lots of people chew wasn't all that keen.
Channel Fourteen was kid's shows all the time,
But you could only watch while eating bowls of slime.

Channels Fifteen and Sixteen were real old movies,
Where actors said things like, "Wow, that's groovy!"
Channel Seventeen was nothing but rocks and dirt,
And some goofy-looking guy in a beard named Kurt.

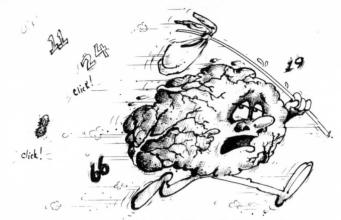

Channel Eighteen was cooking, but it made Tess pout,
'Cause the only thing they cooked was Brussel Sprouts.
Channel Nineteen was All-Croquet,
But you only could watch, they wouldn't let you play.

By the time Tess got to Channel Twenty,
She had seen enough, which was more than plenty.
But her parents said, "No, you have to watch some more,
Our cable goes up to Channel One-Ninety-Four."

"And we have things to do, we're in quite a tizzy,
So, you sit here and watch, it will keep you busy."
And poor Tess had to watch for two whole months,
And she couldn't read a book, and she couldn't move once.

And her brain kind of melted 'cause it was so bored;
It just slid out her ears and down to the floor.
And out to the sidewalk it did ooze and slide,
Looking for a new head to live inside.

Let this be a lesson for you parents and kids;
Don't do what Tess and her folks just did.
Watch one or two channels, not a hundred ninety-four,
Turn the TV off, and go play outdoors.

Read lots of books, maybe paint and draw;
Be the one who 'did', not the one who 'saw'.
Or you'll find, if you can't leave the TV alone,
That your brain may up and run away from home.

MY GIRLFRIEND

I had a girlfriend just last week,
Her name was Polly Beener.
She was real cute, and she liked me,
I wish you could have seen her.

But then I had an argument
With my best friend, T.J.,
He got so mad, to get me back
He stole my girl away.

So now, he gives her notes in class,
And she bought him a scarf;
And every time I look at them,
I think I'm gonna barf.

Is this what grown-ups always feel,
When they say, 'broken heart'?
And mom says, "Time will heal all wounds,"
When is that gonna start?

I miss her writing notes to me,
I miss her hand so warm;
I miss the way she'd run at me
And slug me in the arm.

I know she has the right to go
With anyone she chooses.
I wish T.J.'s heart had the aches
And my arm had the bruises.

THE MOON

The moon's not made of cheese or lard,
It's made of dirt, like my back yard.
It had no face, no man is there.
It can not watch me everywhere.

It's seen no cow jump over it,
No pretty fairies up there sit,
No aliens are hiding there,
And it won't grow a werewolf's hair.

But sometimes, deep inside my heart,
I wish that I was not so smart.
I wish that things were really so,
Like I thought just two years ago.

Then I knew someday I would fly
Inside a rocket, past the sky,
Land on the moon, cut off a piece,
Have a sandwich made of grilled moon cheese.

And then I'd walk around the place,
Leave footprints on the Man-In-The-Moon's face,
And tell him, as I kicked his dirt,
To not watch me when I'm on Earth.

As the cow jumped over the moon and me,
I'd milk it 'cause I was thirsty.
Then I'd hear the moon fairy's silver laughter,
And we'd all live happily ever after.

But I know now it's dirt and rocks and stuff,
And shadows and craters all bumpy and rough;
And there's no air to breathe and one side is all dark;
But I liked it lots better when I wasn't so smart.

27.

ROCKIN' & ROLLIN'

I wanna be a rocker,
I wanna be a roller,
I started playing music
While I was sitting in my stroller.

I wanna live in buses,
I wanna live in campers,
I've been in the music business
Since I started wearing Pampers.

I'm a rock and rollin' baby,
Only eighteen months of age,
If you put me in my walker
I will run out on the stage.

I wanna sell out concerts,
I want to fill some seats,
I've been making audiences happy
Since I was spitting out strained beets.

I wanna hold a guitar,
I want a microphone,
I want to steal my doggie's toy
So I can be Bad To The Bone.

I'm a rock and rollin' baby,
And I'll please the cheering rab
With lyrics like "Goo-goo" and "
And "Plablablabl."

Wanna play some heavy meta
While the groupies push and pu
But it will have to wait 'til later
'Cause right now, my diaper's f

THAD AND THEA

Thad and Thea thought and thought
Of things that they could think in throngs,
They thought of throwing thumbscrews through
Thirty thumping thunderstorms,
Then they thought of threading thistles
Onto thin thimbles and thick thongs.
Thirdly, they thoroughly thought of Thursday
Thwarting three-toed thunderbirds,
And thrashing thugs thusly
By thwacking their thumbs with theatrical thorns
And threatening their thighs with thrown thickets
And thudding thermometers.

Thanks.

'TWAS THE NIGHT--
1994
(with apologies to Clement Clark Moore)

'Twas the night before Christmas, when all through my place,

Not a creature was stirring ('cept this bug on my face);

The stockings were hung on the mantle so handy

In hopes that by morning they'd be all full of candy.

The children were snoring real loud in their beds

While visions of Morphin Power Rangers danced in their heads.

While Ma, in her curlers, mud pack, and perfume,

Got into her bed on her side of the room,

When out on the lawn there arose such a sound,

I thought my big lighted star on the roof just fell down.

Away to the window I quickly did race,

But I stepped on my shoes and I fell on my face.

The moon was so bright you could see it all clear

Like it was daytime at night--man, that was really weird!

When what to my wondering eyes should appear

But some overstuffed sleigh and eight flyin' reindeer;

With a driver who grinned while the sleigh it did bob--

He looked like he's really enjoyin' his job!

They flew like some jet makin' fancy designs,

And he called out to them, tryin' to keep them in line,

"Now, Dasher, look forward; Vixen, listen to me!

Comet, stop punching Cupid—WATCH OUT FOR THAT TREE!!

And, no, Dancer and Donder, we aren't done yet.

We can't stop now, Prancer, you should've gone before we left!"

Like Sonic the Hedgehog, who really can haul,

When he gets goin' fast, just goes straight up a wall,

So, they flew towards my house and went straight up, too,

With the toys and the sleigh and that driver they knew.

Then, in a minute, I heard all them hoofs,

Sounded like they might all just crash right through my roof.

As I ran to the den, with my little dog, Bud,

Down the chimbley Saint Nicholas came with a thud.

He was dressed all in fur from his head to his foot,

Scotchgarded to keep off the ashes and soot.

He got out of the fireplace and grumbled a bit

(He wasn't real happy the fire was still lit!).

His eyes--how they twinkled; his dimples--how merry!

But they were kind of hard to see 'cause his face was so hairy!

He had a white beard and some real long white hair

With the words "Ho! Ho! Ho!" carved in back, right down there!

He was chewin' some gum, and he chewed it real slow

And said, "I gave up my pipe a few years ago."

He had a round face and a big belly, too,

And I said, "I bet Jenny Craig would like to get ahold of you!

And maybe Jane Fonda, or that Richard Simmons guy--

I could see you Sweatin' To The Oldies at the North Pole some night!"

A glare from his eye and a twist of his head,

"Maybe I should put all your toys back up on my sled!"

"No, please, don't do that! Please go on with your work!

Please fill all our stockings! I was being a jerk!"

Well, he did it all quick, like the blink of an eye,

Then back up the chimbley that fellow did fly.

I watched out the window as he signalled them deer;

And, as they hit the sky, he yelled so I could hear,

"It's not good talking ugly--BLITZEN!! WATCH OUT FOR THAT STEEPLE!!

Merry Christmas to all--now, go be nice to people!"

DANCIN' BOBBY

Bobby's parents threw a party
For their grown-up friends downstairs.
He had to stay in his room
Which he didn't think was fair.

They bought him his own pizza
And the videos he liked.
But he wanted to be in the den,
As the Superstar of the Night.

He waited 'til the place filled up,
And the music got real loud,
Then he snuck downstairs and started
Dancing in the middle of the crowd.

He danced for an hour, maybe two,
And everybody cheered.
Then his momma saw who was dancing,
And decorated his rear.

The next weekend, at Bobby's school,
There was a Valentine Dance.
Mom said he was going, for it would
Give his dancing feet their big chance.

On one side of the room were all the boys
On the other, all of the girls.
When the music played, they'd look around
Like they were on two different worlds.

And Bobby just stood there, wearing a tie,
Drinking twenty-six cups of punch.
And the girls just stood in a gaggle,
And the boys all stood in a bunch.

And now, when his folks have a party,
They tell Bobby it's a school affair,
And he sits upstairs, with his movies and pizza,
And never even tries going downstairs.

TREES

I think that I shall never see

A poem lovely as a tree.

Unless that tree's on a science test,

Then I would like the poem best.

34.

ROCKIN' KIDS

We're kids with our own rock & roll band,

Someday we will be the best in the land.

I think we could really light up this town

If we could just figure out what's holding us down.

My name is Katey, I play the drums,

I sing all the songs, except when I hum.

Beside me on stage is my friend Blaze,

And she also sings and has drums that she plays.

Off to my left is a girl named Laura,

She has two drums, but she's getting more tomorrow.

And she sings just as loud as Blaze and me,

It's good that we have mikes for all three.

Behind us is our main drummer, Pam.

And she always plays louder than I am.

Back, next to her, is red-headed Shannon,

She plays her drums like she's shooting a cannon.

We're five rock & rollers with a band of our own

Each time that we play the grown-ups groan.

We've got the beat, and we're loud as can be,

To be a big hit, what else do we need?

35.

NEW RULES DAY

Can we have a rule that, one day of the year,
I get to make rules that we have to use here?

Then on that one day there'd be smiles everyplace,
Cause my first rule's, "Underwear must Be Worn On Your Face."

And, to belch like a pig would not be thought of as rude,
With the rule, "If You Don't Burp, You Don't Get Any Food!"

If you break my next rule at a meal, you must leave,
"You Must Ignore Your Napkin, And Wipe Your Mouth On Your Sleeve."

You must talk in the library, and at movies, too;
Put your hat on your feet, and on your head, a shoe.

If you get a splinter, then you have to laugh;
If they say, "What's your name?" then you must say, "Giraffe!"

If they all sound real weird, made for sillies and fools,
Then imagine all of the trouble I have following your rules!

So, let me have my rules just one day, and no more.
And I'll try to follow yours the other three-hundred-and-sixty-four.

GIRL COLORS

Girl colors are pretty and frilly,

Girl colors are yellow and pink.

Girl colors are like cotton candy,

If you ask me, girl colors stink.

> I am a girl and I wear 'em,
>
> Whenever I go outside and play.
>
> And if I bump into a dirt clod,
>
> You see it from ten feet away.

My mother is always complaining

When I mess up my girl color clothes,

But what if I want to play "jungles"

Or need someplace to wipe my nose?

> Boy clothes are always dark colors
>
> To hide every stain, spot, and scar.
>
> Because of their clothes, boys are always
>
> Twice as dirty as you think they are.

So give me some dark greens and browns

In all of my clothes every day.

And put girl colors just on girl babies

Who never go outside to play.

37.

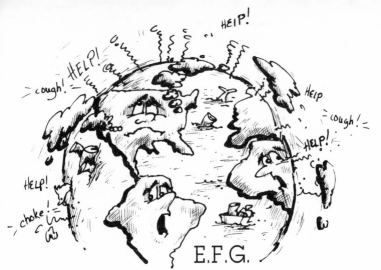

E.F.G.

Earth Fixing Guy, he's the Earth Fixing Guy;
He knows how to swim and he knows how to fly.
He knows how to sing and he knows how to surf;
But mainly, he knows how to fix up the Earth.

His partner is known as the Earth Fixing Gal;
If you're kind to the Earth, she is always your pal.
But if you are a person who likes to pollute,
She might give you a triple-back-kick in the snoot.

He eats right, and works out, and never gets sick;
He makes Arnold Schwarzenegger look like a toothpick.
She is so strong and good, she is never a meanie;
She makes Supergirl seem like a wimp-headed weenie.

They clean up the land and they clean up the sea;
On their chest is a crest that reads "E-F-G"!
And, just like your room, when you let it get junky,
Our Earth's getting dirty, and moldy, and funky.

Earth Fixing Guy says, "Our water's in trouble;
Filled with such toxic wastes, you could walk on the bubbles.
Our rivers are turning to greenish-brown sludge;
That tastes like dead-fish-and-rotten-frog fudge!"

Earth Fixing Gal says, "Yes, our rivers aren't pretty,
But take a sniff of the air around any big city!
The factories and cars have hurled out such a hot haze
That your nose wishes it was on the inside of your face!"

But, these two E.F.G. folks, no matter how strong,
If they work without stopping, all the week long,
Couldn't fix every problem, they can't cover the distance.
For the Earth to get fixed, they'll need some assistance.

So, if Earth's destruction is making you mad,
And you want to help fix the only planet we've had--
Put an "E.F.G." patch on your chest or your pocket;
And go 'round your neighborhood, fast as a rocket.

Recycle, clean trash up, or stop some pollution.
Then you are a part of the Earth Fixing Solution.
If enough folks become Earth Fixing Gals and Guys,
Then millions of hands could help Earth de-toxify.

Sometime in the future, when we've healed our Earth's hurts,
All the people will wear "E.F.G.'s" on their shirts;
When our planet is healthy, on that future date,
Then "E.F.G." will be standing for "Earth Feels Great!"   39.

FRIEDA'S FOOTBALL GAME

As the kids all gathered 'round
For the first game of the fall,
The goal was Beat The Other Team,
The game it was...football.
The captains picked their teams
They knew their pals by heart.
They'd gotten bigger since last year,
Some might have gotten smart.
'Til only one was left--a new kid who wasn't going to play.
Plus she was a girl...and she was little...and that was all they had to say

So Frieda stood there, angry,
Trying not to pout or cry;
She wanted in the football game,
And they did not know why.
This was a rough and tumble game
Each weekend every fall.
And Frieda looked like she'd lose
A wrestling match with a Barbie doll.
And they didn't want to hurt her, so they wished she'd go away.
Plus she was a girl...and she was little...and that was all they had to say.

For two hours they played football
Like the pro scouts were in view;
Six bloody noses happened
And three eyes went black and blue,
And seven heads got great big knots,
And one kid swallowed mud,
And every boy thought it was great--
The bruises, dirt, and blood.
But tiny Frieda stood there, waiting for her chance to play.
But she was a girl...and she was little...and that was all they had to say.

One minute left in game time
When came the worst cut of all;
Halfback Peter Pooper's mother
Gave her son a dinner call.
The score was tied when he left,
Would his team forfeit the game?
The boys all looked at Frieda,
And one whispered out her name.
Yes, they would lose the game without her, so they had to let her play;
But she was a girl...and she was little...and that was all they had to say.

Well, Mookie hiked to Mudface,
And Mudface turned to pass,
But his feet slipped in the mud
And the football hit the grass.
All the boys went diving for it
Like it was a greasy pig;
But the ball skidded and bounced to
Two hands that were not very big.
Frieda looked at boys twice her size, and now they would make her pay;
Though she was a girl...and she was little...and that was all they had to say

She grabbed the first boy by his shirt
And lifted him up off the ground
And he flew eight or nine feet
And landed with a thudding sound.
First one boy, and then another
She picked up and threw out of her way.
She left them lying on the field
As she scored and saved the day.

They couldn't wait until next week so they could be on Frieda's team;
Yes, she was a girl...and she was little...
But she was the strongest kid they'd ever seen!

Touchdown!

41.

PLEASE AIM YOUR FOOD CAREFULLY

My baby brother really
Gets excited when he eats.
Sitting in his high chair
Digging into mashed-up beets.

But he never hits his mouth
Although it's very big.
So all around his high chair
Is like the home of a pig.

He flips each spoonful up
But usually it will fall
Back past his fuzzy head
And wind up on the wall.

Mom saw how much he liked
Watching us play video games,
So she drew targets on him
To help improve his aim.

For every time he landed food
Inside of either ear,
He got seven bonus points
And everybody cheered.

If the top of his head
Is where his veggies land,
Ten more points go on the board
And we give him a hand.

And if his eyes collect
Big blobs of applesauce;
He gets another twenty points,
And even more applause.

If beets run up his nose
And cause quite a sensation.
We give him fifty points plus
A family standing ovation.

His mouth's the prize to hit
With any food at all
He gets one hundred points and a
Parade right down the hall.

We've played this for two months;
He still can't find his face.
It's like he had a force-field
Around his head someplace.

He's got no points or applause
From us, and that's no bull;
And though his stomach's very empty
Our walls are getting full.

I THINK THAT MY MOTHER IS MAGIC

I think that my mother is magic,
Like a fairy, a troll, or an elf.
But, let me just tell you what happened
And you can decide for yourself.

For all of my life she has hollered
At the mess I have made in my room.
'Til last Thursday evening she told me
It was time that she "lowered the boom".

I don't even know what a 'boom' is,
And I didn't know it was up high,
But if I hear one more is coming,
I'll go hide in the blink of an eye.

Well, my mother went up in the attic,
And came down wearing Grandma's old dress.
And she drew a broom using some sparkles
In the middle of all of my mess.

And she mumbled some words that I heard
On a Disney cartoon once or twice.
And the flash on my floor looked like lightning
And I ran and I covered my eyes.

When I came back my room was lots weirder,
There were coat-hooks all over my floor,
And my bed was inside of my closet,
And there were suction cups on my door.

Now, when I go in my bedroom,
And I throw my clothes down on the floor,
They hang themselves up on the coat-hooks,
And they don't even smell any more.

If I try to hang stuff in my closet
(Which is hard, with my bed shoved in there),
My clothes just fly right off the hangers,
To my coat-hook-floor... it isn't fair!

As I walk in, my door's suction cups,
Pull the hat and the shoes off of me;
And I have to walk in on my walls now,
Since my floor is as neat as can be.

And my Mother just sits, smiling strangely,
Still wearing my Grandma's old dress.
And I just heard her telling my Father
That she thinks the whole house is a mess.

If she makes the house work like my bedroom,
Then a theme park is next in the plan,
And maybe we'd call it Weird Gardens,
Or Six Flags Over Loony Mom Land.

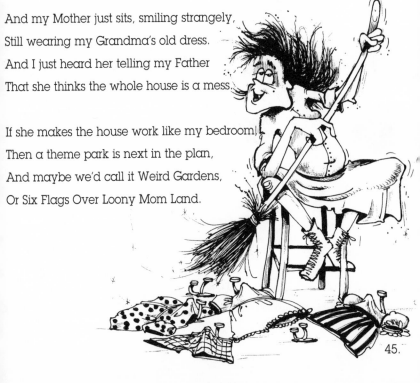

45.

BOOM!!

"If you eat more pie, you'll burst!"
Said John's mom at lunch one day.
"OK!" said little Johnny,
"Pass the pie and get out of the way!!"

MOSQUITO BITE

My arm got a mosquito bite,
My mother said, "Scratch it not!
Or it will get infected and will
Bleed and leak a lot!"

Well, every time I looked,
My fingers were a-twitching;
Trying to sneak up on that dot
Causing all my itching.

I put socks on my hands,
Then put them in my pockets.
But still they tried to rub the bite,
I thought the socks would stop it.

I got my friend to tape my hands
Against my legs real tight.
But still they kept on trying
To reach that mosquito bite.

I tried to rub against a tree,
I fell and rolled downhill.
I hit thorn bushes and a rock
They called it, "quite a spill."

My arm broke in two places;
It's purple and it's sore.
But, one good thing, at least
It isn't itching any more!

47.

UNCLE DENTIST

My uncle was a dentist once,
They called him Hank the Slammer,
He never, ever used a drill--
He always used a hammer.

And if you had a cavity,
He'd knock it out of you.
If you wanted to be put to sleep,
He'd use the hammer, too.

But, once he whacked a governor
Hard with his dental hammer.
Now he just sits and dreams of teeth,
In a jail in Alabama.

AM I GREAT, OR WHAT?

I'm bigger than you,

I'm better than you,

I'm cuter than should be allowed.

I'm smarter than you,

I'm politer than you,

My parents should both be so proud.

I'm faster than you,

I'm stronger than you,

I'm the newest kid here in this town.

I'm neater than you,

I'm cooler than you,

When I dance, everybody sits down.

I'm prouder than you,

I'm louder than you,

If you sit here, I'll put on a show,

I'm funnier than you,

I act better than you--

Hey, wait!! Where did everyone go?

BIG FAMILY

Is anybody else out there
A kid who's been divorced?
I thought I was the only one
But I keep meeting more.

The sad part is, I miss my dad,
Each month I see him twice.
But, when birthdays and Christmas come,
That's when it's really nice.

Mom has remarried, Dad has, too,
That's lots of family.
I think I've got twelve grandparents
And they all buy gifts for me.

I've got cousins, aunts, and uncles,
I think there's forty-eight.
And three of them are famous,
But, they live in other states.

50.

Mom and Dad could keep on
getting more and more divorces,
know somehow I'd end up
vings cousins with farms and horses.

nd grandparents by the hundreds
uying presents by the dozens;
nd I know one day I'd wake up
nd find I was my own cousin.

ut, if Mom and Dad kept going
n this divorce-and-marriage spin,
hen they might accidentally
larry each other once again.

d be back where I started,
randparents who total four,
lo cousins, one ugly brother--
hat would really be a bore!

VOMITUS INTERRUPTUS

(Also known as "The Ralph Poem")

Listen my children, both north and south,
Of the mid-day visit from my dear friend Ralph.
It was in January, just past New Year's,
All of the schoolkids were gathered here.

I said to the kids, "If you like the show,
There are two ways you can let me know.
One is by hand, and two is by cheer;
First, clap if it's good, so I can hear."

"The second is cheering, if it's great;
But, cheer right away, don't make me wait.
So, cheer with your mouth and your hand and your arm,
So they hear you in each nearby village and farm."

So, I started in with "Good Morning!"--loud!
And the echo came back from that happy crowd.
Just as the principal stood 'cross the way,
I hollered out poems to brighten their day.

Some poems were good, and they gave me a hand;
And I got loud cheers for the ones that were grand.
But, just as one poem was leaving my mouth,
Some girl in the middle let out a loud "Ralph!!"

From the stage I watched, as this poor girl,
Recalling her breakfast, began to hurl.
I was hoping she had caught some kind of a flu
And wasn't saying, "Mr. Poet, here's what I think of you!"

I tried to continue, to joke and to shout,
While the kids all around her began to spread out.
Soon a big empty circle grew up, like a flame,
With this girl in the middle, still calling Ralph's name.

en the principal came, with some great big wet towels,
st as she finished purging her bowels.
en the maintenance engineer arrived with a mop,
nd the entire assembly ground to a stop.

e nurse takes the girl, as her fever increases;
nd some boy in the fifth grade asks for the big pieces;
e floor was soon clean, and the kids settled in,
nd the assembly got back to full weirdness again.

ow, I've done assemblies with colds in my head;
nd I've had to yell when the speakers went dead;
e had to read poems while jet planes roared;
nd I even did one where the principal snored.

it, in my history, I hope I won't know
ny more days when I must stop my show
cause a mid-morning message from some poor girl's mouth
ys, "Hey, stop reading poems while I'm calling Ralph!"

special thanks for the idea, title, and encouragement to my friend
Nancy Lou Cheshire McWatters Rosenblatt)

53.

PUD MUDDLE

Mom told me,
"Don't get wet!"
I heard her clear as clear could be.
But when I got
Halfway home,
There was a pud muddle in front of me.

It looked wide,
But not deep,
I jumped to splash the water away.
I sank in
Up to my knees--
I'm already wet, so I guess I'll play.

Pud muddle ears,
Pud muddle clothes,
Pud muddle in my mouth and hair.
New white shoes
Are brownish-gray,
Pud muddle in my underwear.

I got home,
Mom passed out;
Sent me up to bathe and scrub.
I got in,
Was so dirty,
I made a pud muddle in my tub!

What I learned
About pud muddles
Is something that I'd like to share--
Once you get
Dirty enough,
You can take a pud muddle everywhere!

THE DREAM

you're going to dream such a wonderful dream,
s you're lying asleep in your bed,
hat a smile's on your face as you're first waking up
rom the dream that is still in your head.

nd if nobody else seems to quite understand;
o explain it, you practically shout it;
you really did dream such a wonderful dream,
hen go out and do something about it.

you dream you're a rock star, start learning to play,
nd someday, you'll be up in those lights.
you dream you can fly, you know, you just might,
s a pilot on Space Shuttle flights.

you dream you're the President, start campaigning now,
earn how government works, and you'll be there.
you dream climbing mountains, practice now on dirt hills,
nd someday, you'll tell us all you see there.

you're going to dream such a wonderful dream
hat it makes you feel great through and through,
hen get out of your bed with that dream in your head,
nd start now, and you'll make it come true.

(This is a quiet and
serious poem, kind of like
the cool-down at the end of a hard workout.)

INDEX BY TITLE